What Is It?

by Timothy Andrews
Illustrated by Leanne Franson

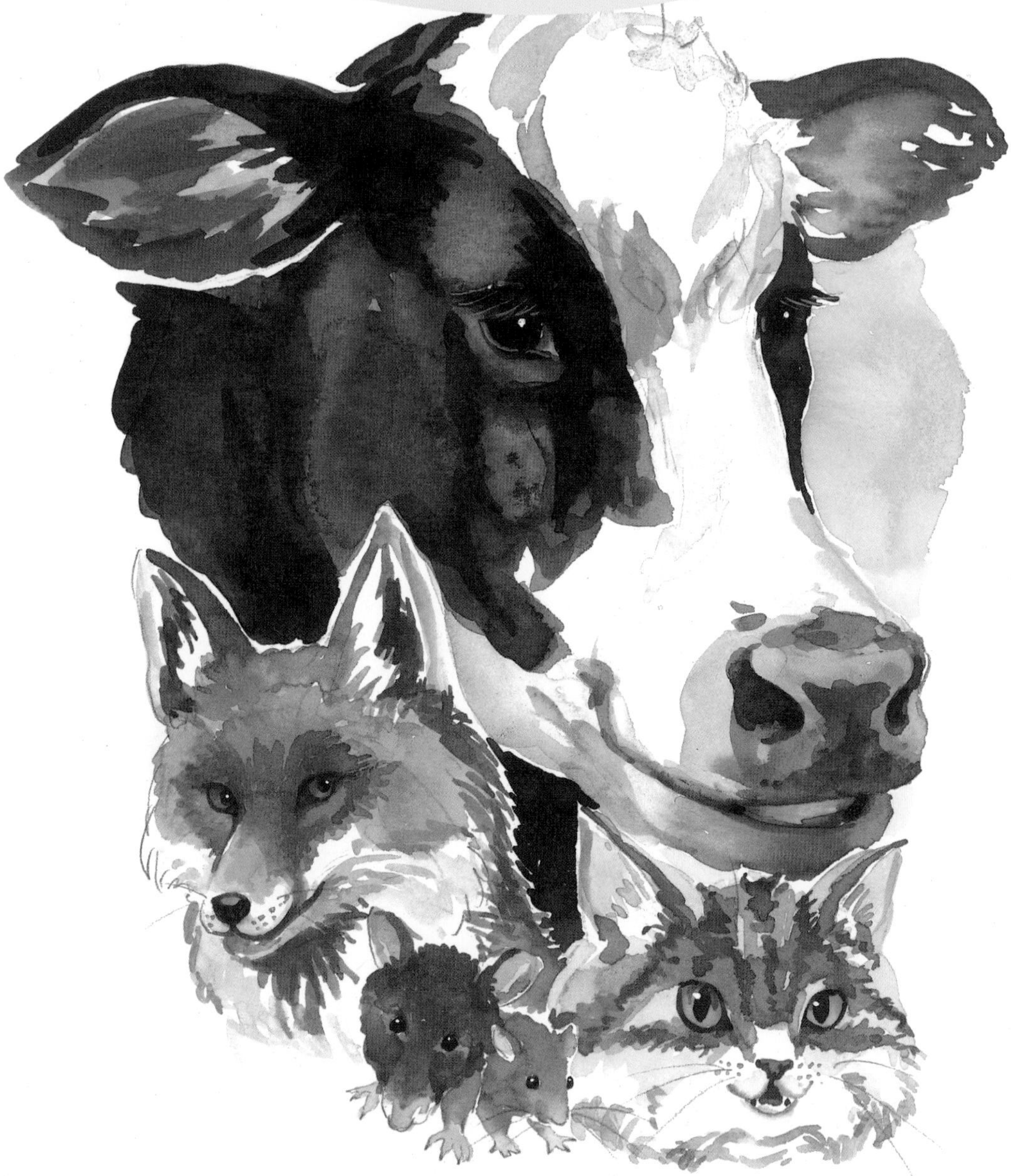

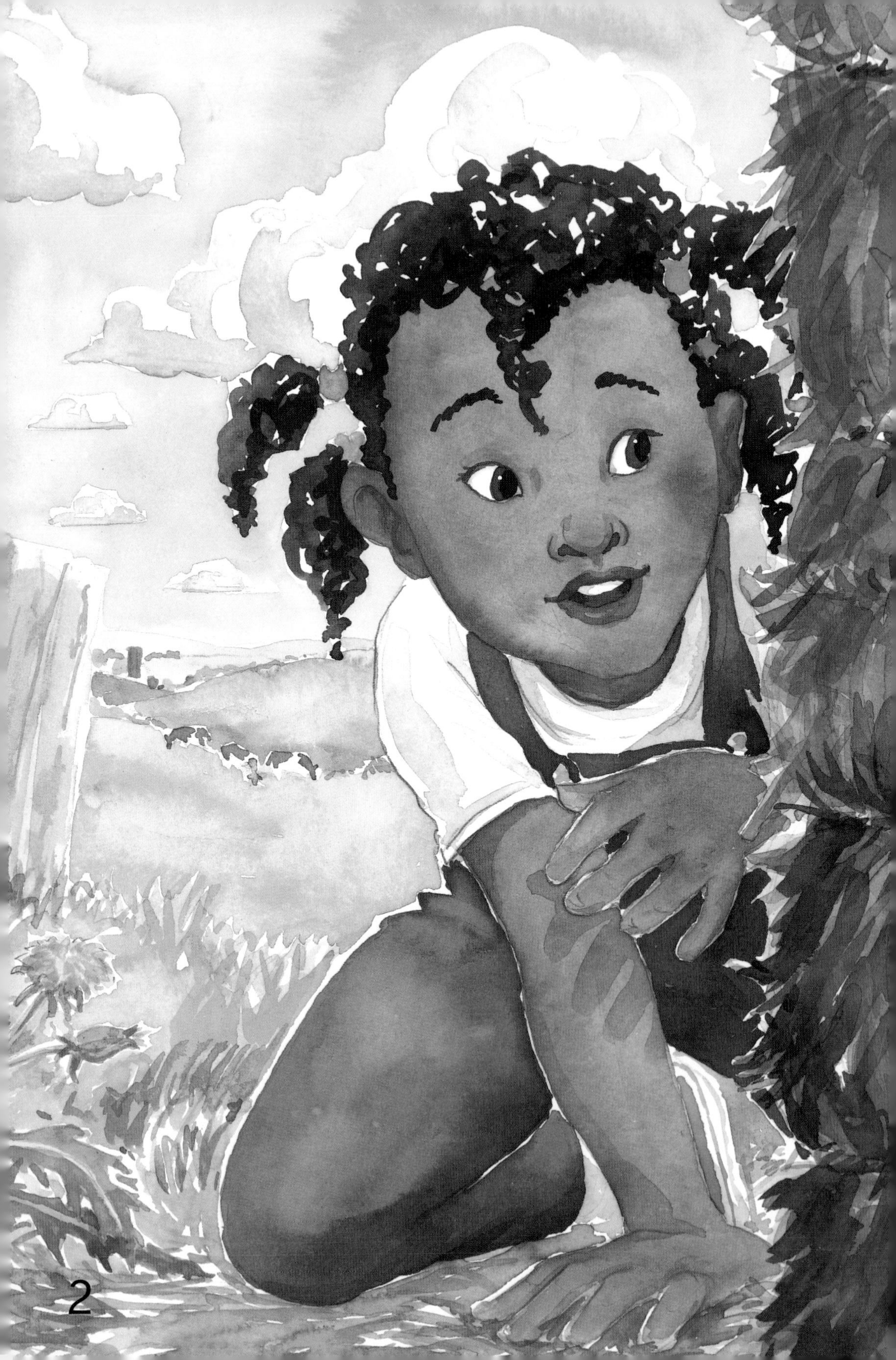

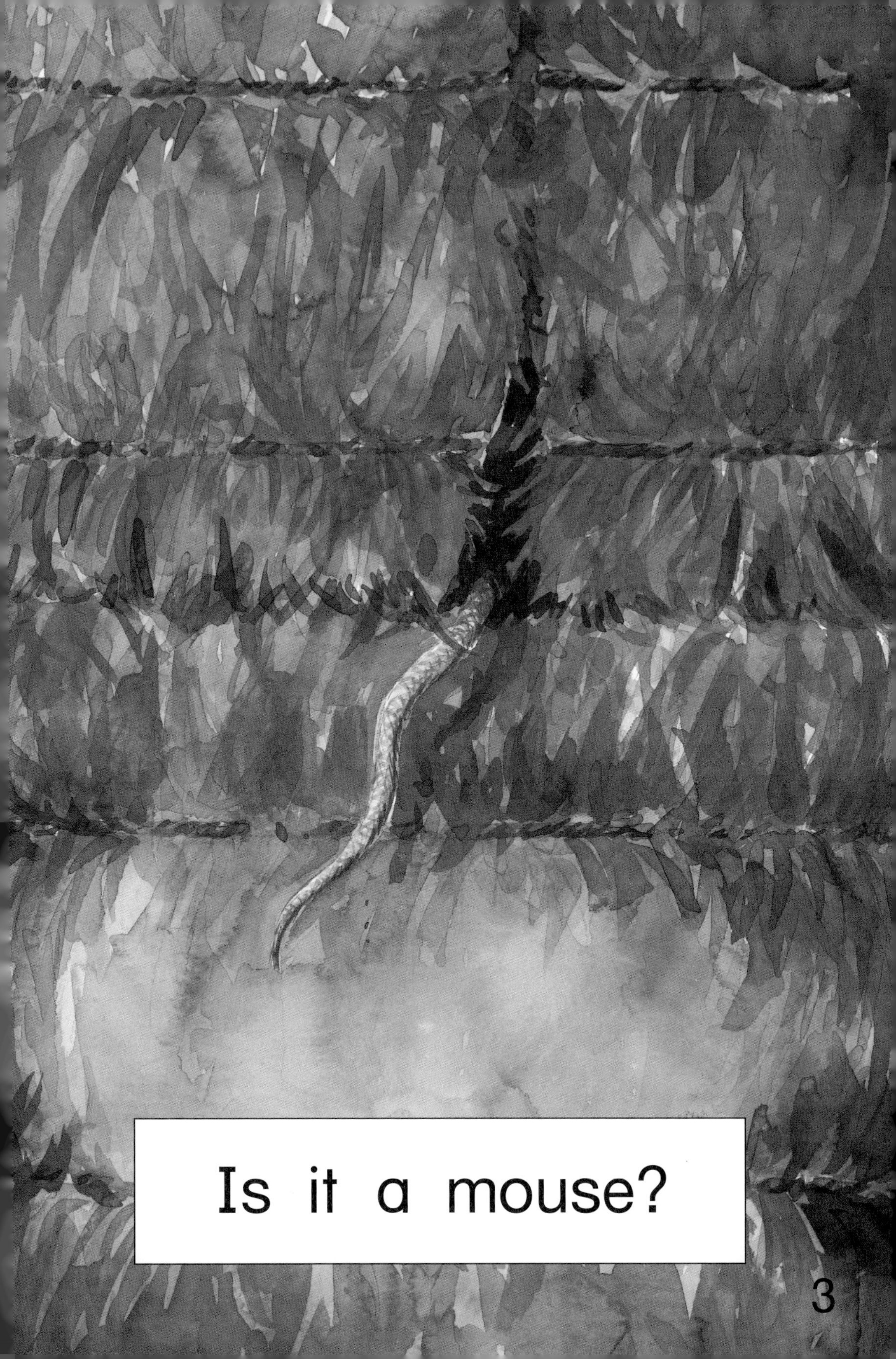

Is it a mouse?

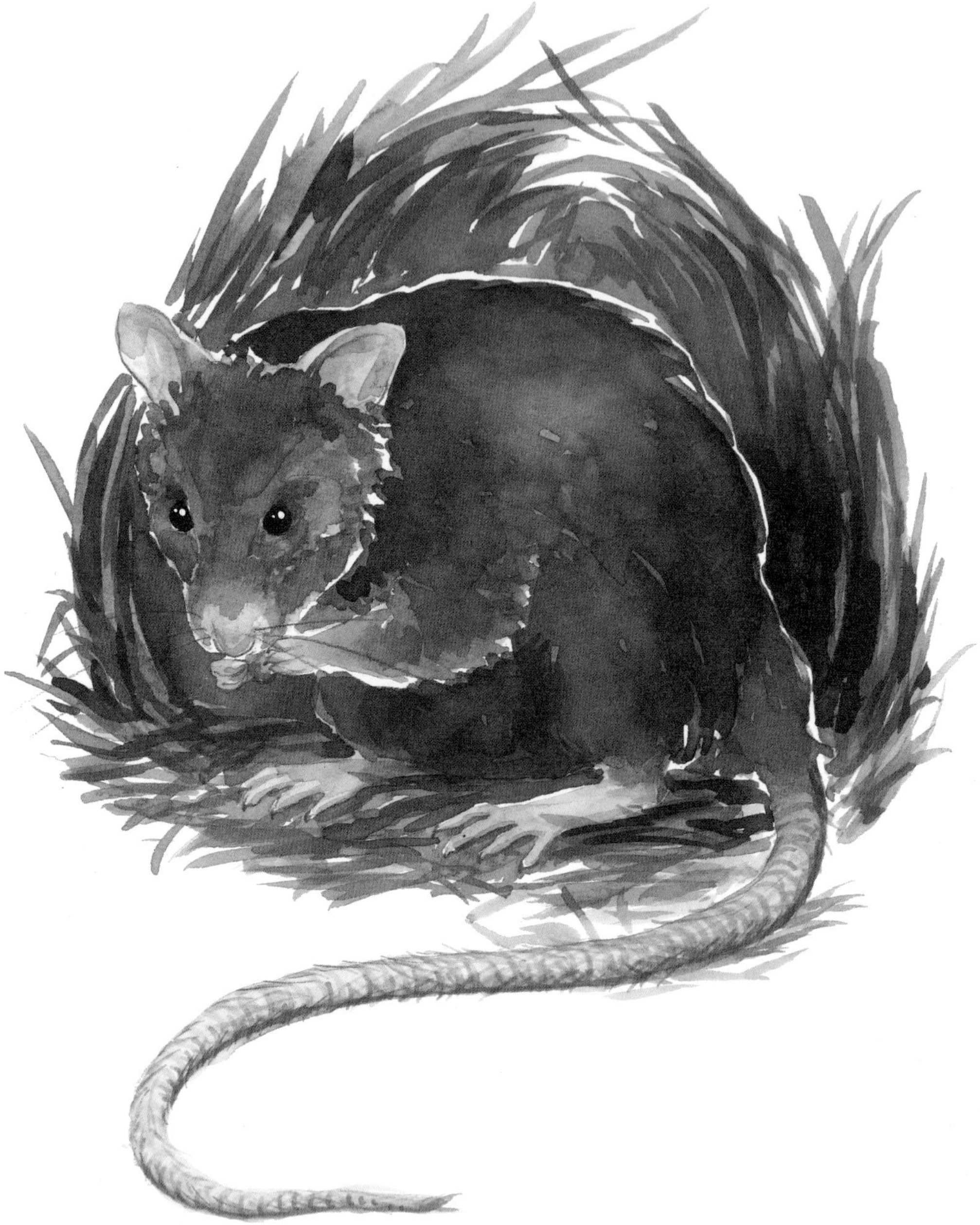

No, it's a rat.

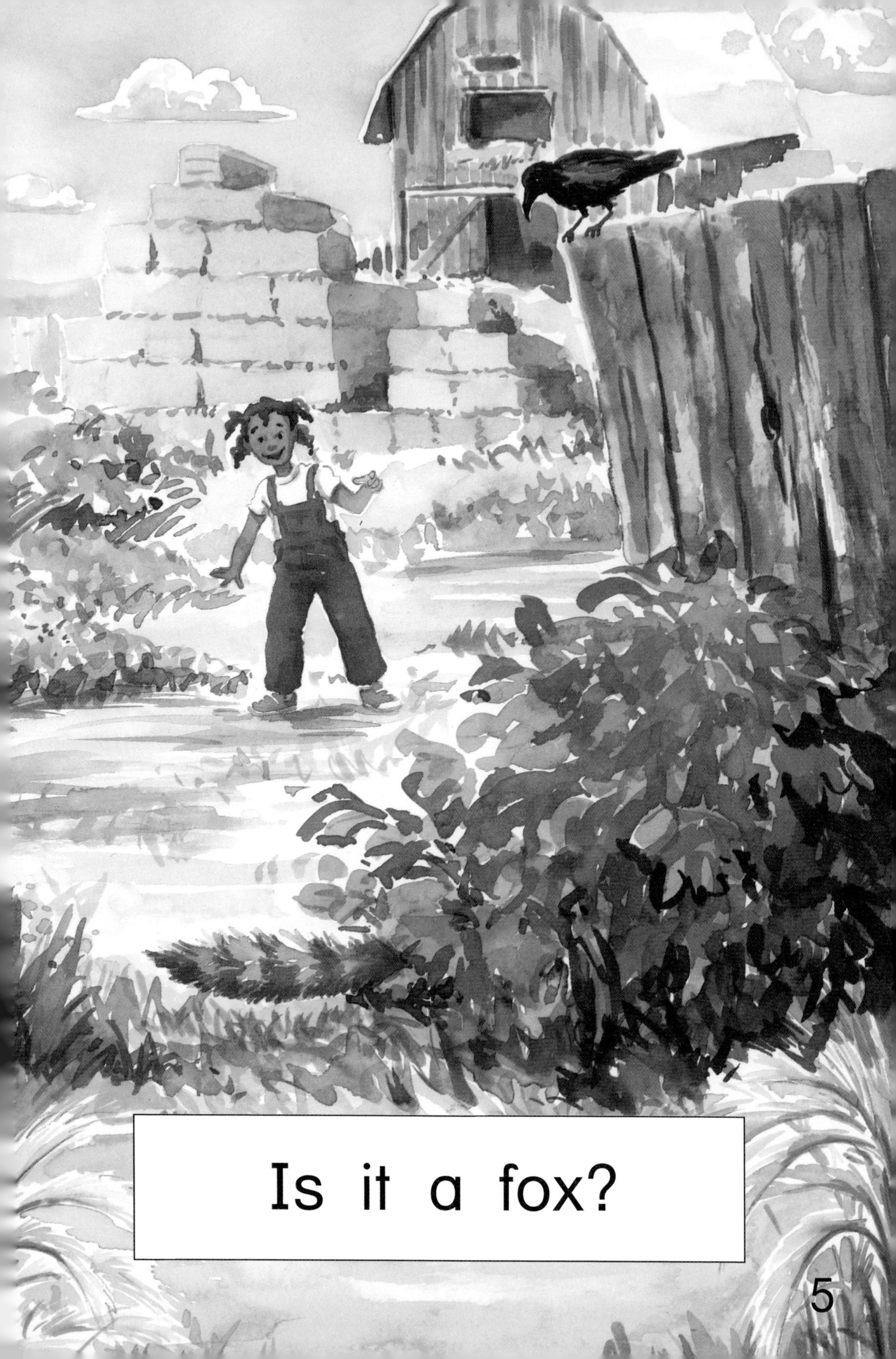

Is it a fox?

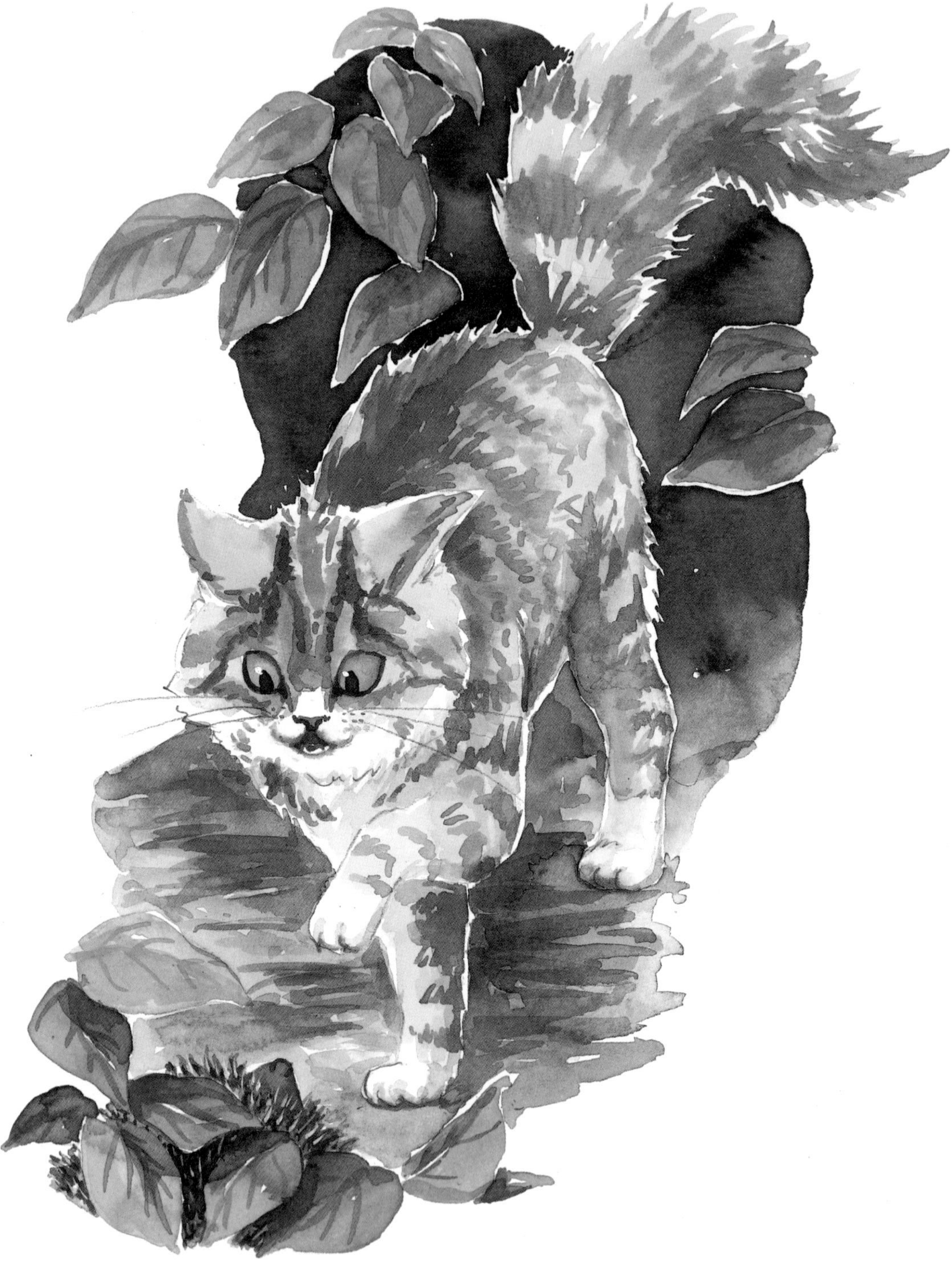

No, it's a cat.

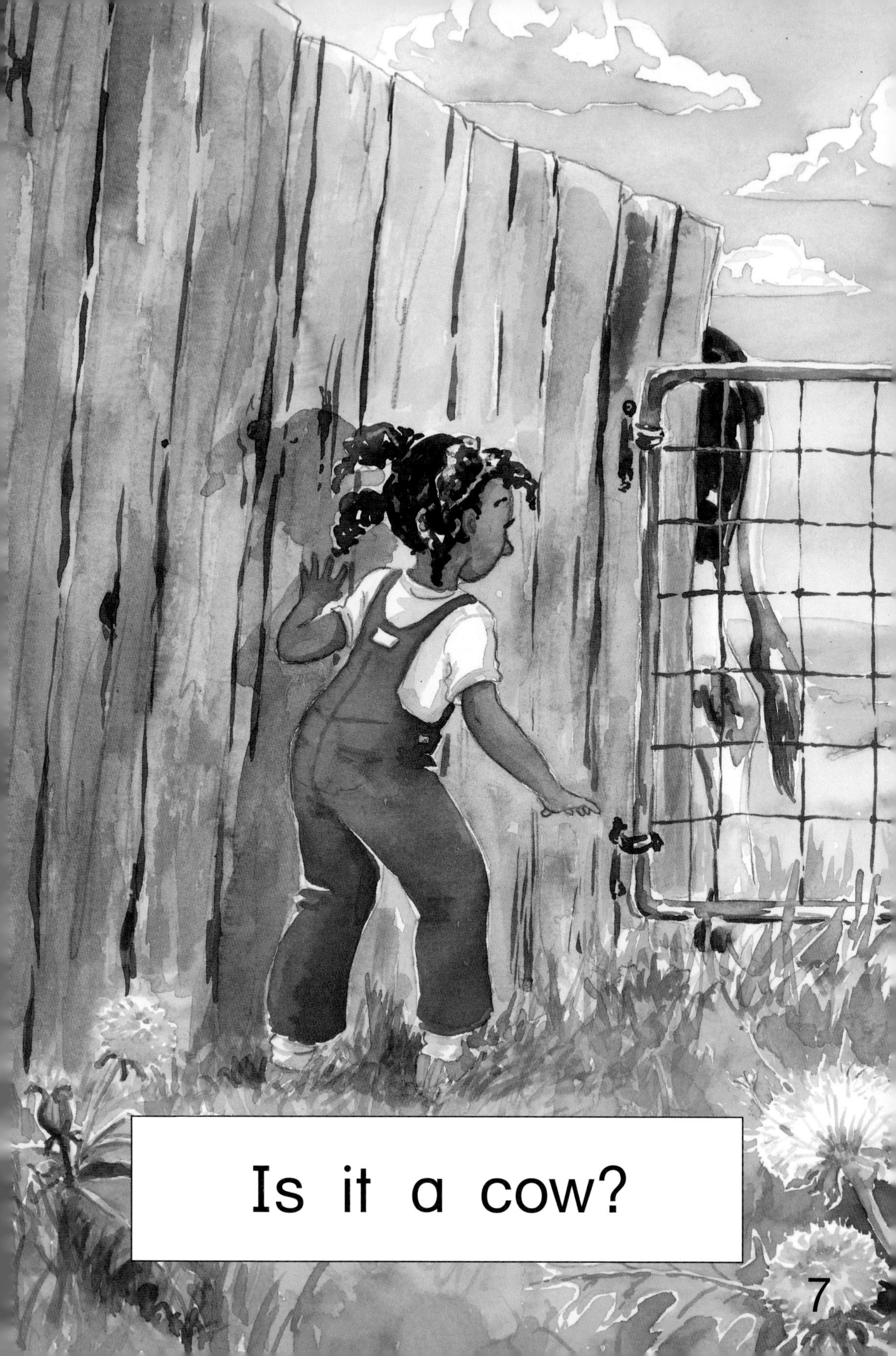

Is it a cow?

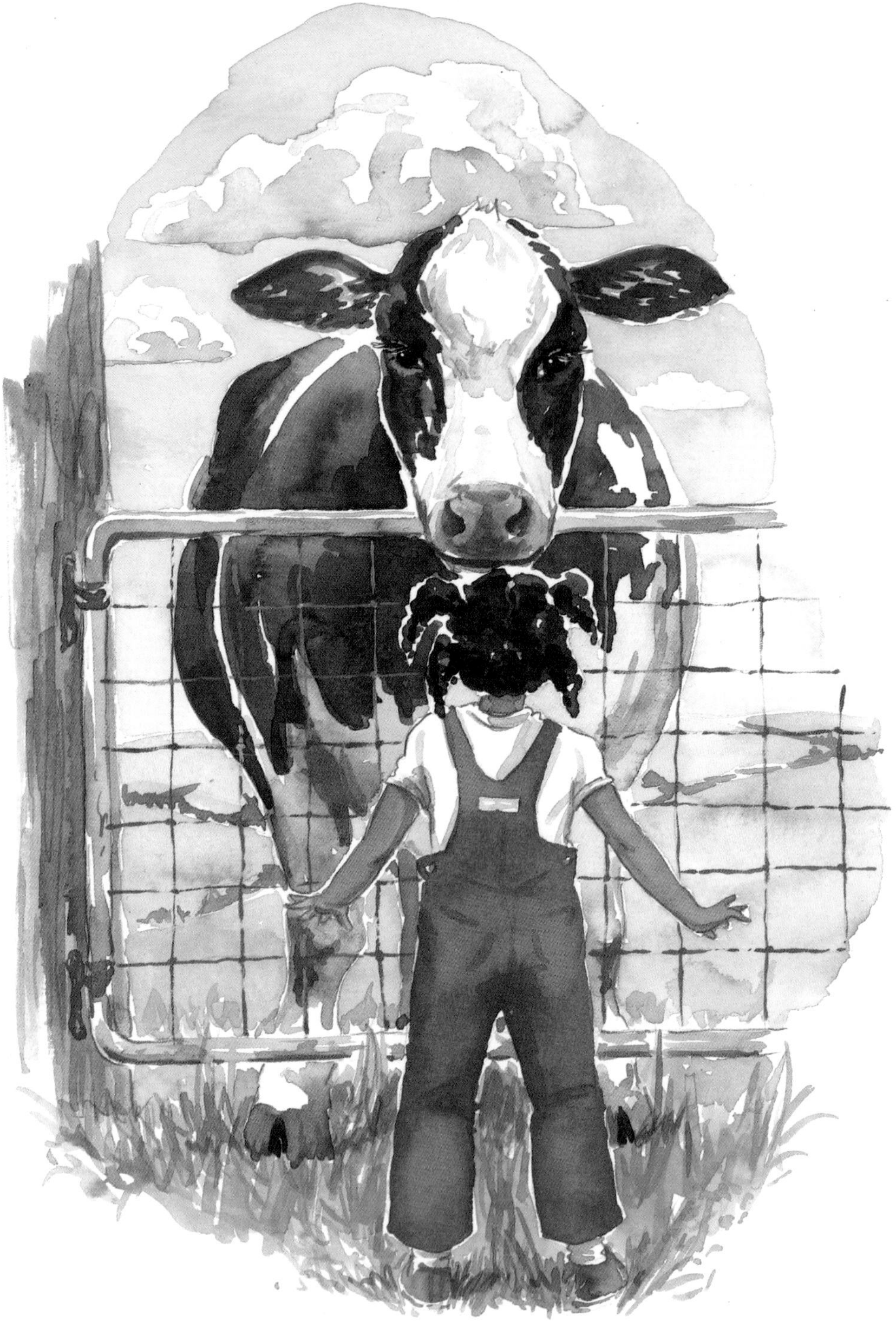

Yes! Wow!